NEW FROM DAVE BROWNE

MOVING TO THE HEAD OF LIFE'S CLASS

	FAITH
FRIENDS	
FAMILY	
	WITH STRAIGHT F'S
	FITNESS
FUN	

MOVING TO THE HEAD OF LIFE'S CLASS

FIVE FACTORS FOR SUCCESSFUL LIVING

	FAITH
FRIENDS	
FAMILY	
	WITH STRAIGHT F'S
	FITNESS
FUN	

The quoted ideas expressed in this book (but not scripture verses) are not, in all cases, exact quotations, as some have been edited for clarity and brevity. In all cases, the author has attempted to maintain the speaker's original intent. In some cases, quoted material for this book was obtained from secondary sources, primarily print media. While every effort was made to ensure the accuracy of these sources, the accuracy cannot be guaranteed. For additions, deletions, corrections or clarifications in future editions of this text, please write ELM HILL BOOKS.

Scripture quotations are taken from.

The Holy Bible, New International Version (NIV) Copyright © 1973, 1978, 1984, by International Bible Society. Used by permission of Zondervan Publishing House. All rights reserved.

The Holy Bible, New King James Version (NKJV) Copyright © 1982 by Thomas Nelson, Inc. Used by permission.

The New American Standard Bible®, (NASB) Copyright © 1960, 1962, 1963, 1968, 1971, 1972, 1973, 1975, 1977, 1995 by The Lockman Foundation. Used by permission.

The Message(MSG) Copyright © by Eugene H. Peterson 1993, 1994,1995. Used by permission of NavPress Publishing Group.

Cover Design by Karen Phillips
Page Layout by Bart Dawson

Special Assistance from Tim Way

ISBN 1-4041-8445-7

Printed in the United States of America

TABLE OF CONTENTS

THE FIVE F'S:

AN INTRODUCTION BY DAVE BROWNE

In school, the ultimate goal is straight A's: acing the tests, making the honor roll, and earning the perfect report card. But in life *beyond* the classroom, I firmly believe that it takes five F's to move to the head of the class. These five factors are, in fact, the key to the victorious life God promises each of us.

I have shared the "5-F's" principle on many occasions with family members and friends. Recently, I used it as the theme for a speech I delivered to my associates at Family Christian Stores. The book you now hold in your hands is an expansion of that speech.

As Christians, we are comforted by the promise of John 10:10: "I have come that they may have life, and that they may have it more abundantly" (NKJV). But as believers we must beware: while God promises us *the opportunity* for abundance, He does not *guarantee it*. We human beings are creatures of free will; as such, we are free to claim God's gifts—or not. This text is intended as a general guidebook and a personal roadmap for claiming those gifts. I do not, by any means, profess to have life "all figured out." It was simply laid on my heart to share the "5-F's" and what they have meant to me, for they provide direction to the abundant life.

The successful life begins and ends with faith in God and faith in Jesus Christ. Faith is the cornerstone in the foundation of a well-lived life. Building on the cornerstone of faith, I maintain that at least four other factors lead to a balanced, healthy, happy life. These factors are family, fitness, friends, and fun.

Do you sincerely seek to claim the abundance God offers His believers? If so, the following pages—compiled and edited by my friends at Elm Hill Books and J. Countryman—can most certainly help. As you consider the Bible verses, quotations, and essays that follow, remember that God has glorious gifts in store for you. May you accept His blessings with open arms. May He, in turn, richly bless you and yours.

So here's to your life's next report card—may it be filled with "F's.

Dave Browne,
CEO, Family Christian Stores

F AS IN FAITH

FAITH

FRIENDS

FAMILY

But without faith it is impossible to please Him, for he who comes to God must believe that He is, and that He is a rewarder of those who diligently seek Him. Hebrews 11:6 NKJV

FITNESS

FUN

FAITH

A successful life begins—and ends—with faith: faith in God, faith in God's promises, and faith in God's Son. If we place our lives in God's hands, our faith is rewarded in ways that we—as human beings with clouded vision and limited understanding—can scarcely comprehend.

My parents provided the direction to find my faith by being great examples and pushing me towards church. "If you can stay out and play, you can get up and pray . . ." was a regular Sunday morning wake-up nudge at our house. However, faith is not just found. It is a journey of discovery and growth, and the source of true hope and joy.

Do you desire the abundance and success God has promised? Then trust Him today and every day you live. Trust Him with every aspect of your life. Trust His promises. Trust in the saving grace of His only begotten Son. Then, when you have entrusted your future to the Giver of all things good, rest assured that your future is secure, not only for today, but also for all eternity.

CHAPTER 1: FAITH IN OUR CREATOR

FAITH

FRIENDS

FAMILY

If you have faith as a mustard seed, you will say to this mountain, 'Move from here to there,' and it will move; and nothing will be impossible for you. Matthew 17:20 NKJV

FITNESS

FUN

Every life—including yours—is a series of successes and failures, celebrations and disappointments, joys and sorrows. Every step of the way, through every triumph and tragedy, God will stand by your side and strengthen you *if* you have faith in Him. Jesus taught his disciples that if they had faith, they could move mountains. You can too.

When a suffering woman sought healing by merely touching the hem of His cloak, Jesus replied, "Daughter, be of good comfort; thy faith hath made thee whole" (Matthew 9:24 KJV). The message to believers of every generation is clear: we must live by faith today and every day.

When you place your faith, your trust, indeed your life in the hands of Your Heavenly Father, you'll be amazed at the marvelous things He can do with you and through you. So strengthen your faith through praise, through worship, through Bible study, and through prayer. Trust God's plans. With Him, all things are possible, and He stands ready to open a world of possibilities to you . . . *if* you have faith.

Faith in God is a terrific venture in the dark.
Oswald Chambers

Faith is greater than learning
Martin Luther

Faith means being grasped by a power that is
greater than we are, a power that shakes us
and turns us, and transforms and heals us.
To surrender to this power is faith.
Paul Tillich

Understanding is the reward of faith.
Therefore, seek not to understand that
you may believe, but believe that
you may understand.
St. Augustine

"JESUS SAID TO HIM, 'IF YOU CAN BELIEVE, ALL THINGS ARE POSSIBLE TO HIM WHO BELIEVES.'"

Mark 9:23 NKJV

When you believe that nothing significant
can happen through you, you have said
more about your belief in God
than you have said about yourself.
Henry Blackaby

If all things are possible with God,
then all things are possible to him
who believes in him.
Corrie ten Boom

The impossible is exactly what God does.
Oswald Chambers

Following God will require faith and action.
Without faith you will not be able
to please God. When you act in faith,
God is pleased.
Henry Blackaby and Claude King

Faith means believing in realities that go
beyond sense and sight. It is the awareness of
unseen divine realities all around you.
Joni Eareckson Tada

Faith is stronger than fear.
John Maxwell

That we may not complain of what is,
let us see God's hand in all events; and,
that we may not be afraid of what shall be,
let us see all events in God's hand.
Matthew Henry

The strengthening of faith comes from staying
with it in the hour of trial. We should not
shrink from tests of faith.
Catherine Marshall

Having faith in God doesn't mean that
everything is going to go your way. It simply
means that you will have his peace and
joy on those days when you wonder
why you ever got out of bed!
Pat Williams

ONLY GOD CAN MOVE MOUNTAINS, BUT FAITH AND PRAYER CAN MOVE GOD.

E. M. Bounds

"I CAN DO ALL THINGS THROUGH HIM WHO STRENGTHENS ME."

Philippians 4:13 NASB

CHAPTER 2: FAITH IN GOD'S PLAN

FAITH

FRIENDS

FAMILY

The counsel of the LORD stands forever, the plans of His heart to all generations.
Psalm 33:11 NKJV

FITNESS

FUN

God has a plan for everything, including you. But God won't force His plans upon you. To the contrary, He has given you free will, the ability to make decisions on your own. With the freedom to choose, comes the responsibility of living with the consequences of those choices.

If you seek to live in accordance with God's will for your life—and you should—then you must trust in the grand design of your Heavenly Father. You must live in accordance with His commandments. You must study God's Word and be watchful for His signs. If you seek to know God's will for your life, you should associate with fellow Christians who will encourage your spiritual growth. You should listen to the inner voice that speaks to you in the quiet moments of your daily devotionals.

Have you entrusted your life to God's plan, or have you resisted Him? Have you trusted God's perfect will, or have you sought—in vain—to impose your own will upon the world? God intends to use you in wonderful, unexpected ways *if* you let Him. The decision to seek God's plan and to follow it is yours and yours alone. The consequences of that decision have implications both profound and eternal, so choose carefully.

The Almighty does nothing without reason,
although the frail mind of man cannot
explain the reason.
St. Augustine

God surrounds you with opportunity.
You and I are free in Jesus Christ,
not to do whatever we want, but to be
all that God wants us to be.
Warren Wiersbe

God will not permit any troubles to come
upon us unless He has a specific plan
by which great blessing can
come out of the difficulty.
Peter Marshall

We are uncertain of the next step,
but we are certain of God.
Oswald Chambers

*For now we see in a mirror, dimly, but then face
to face. Now I know in part, but
then I shall know just as I also am known.*
1 Corinthians 13:12 NKJV

*O Lord of hosts, Blessed is the man
who trusts in You!*
Psalms 84:12 NKJV

Every experience God gives us,
every person he puts in our lives,
is the perfect preparation for the future
that only he can see.
Corrie ten Boom

GOD ISN'T A TALENT SCOUT LOOKING FOR SOMEONE WHO IS "GOOD ENOUGH" OR "STRONG ENOUGH." HE IS LOOKING FOR SOMEONE WITH A HEART SET ON HIM, AND HE WILL DO THE REST.

Vance Havner

Number one, God brought me here. It is by
His will that I am in this place. In that fact
I will rest. Number two, He will keep me here
in His love and give me grace to behave as
His child. Number three, He will make
the trial a blessing, teaching me the lessons
He intends for me to learn and working in me
the grace He means to bestow. Number four,
in His good time He can bring me out again.
How and when, He knows.
So, let me say I am here.

Andrew Murray

God possesses infinite knowledge and an
awareness which is uniquely His. At all times,
even in the midst of any type of suffering,
I can realize that He knows, loves, watches,
understands, and more than that,
He has a purpose.

Billy Graham

When the dream of our heart is one that God has planted there, a strange happiness flows into us. At that moment, all of the spiritual resources of the universe are released to help us. Our praying is then at one with the will of God and becomes a channel for the Creator's purposes for us and our world.

Catherine Marshall

When you become consumed by God's call on your life, everything will take on new meaning and significance. You will begin to see every facet of your life—including your pain—as a means through which God can work to bring others to Himself.

Charles Swindoll

God's will is not given to us for our approval;
it is given to us for our acceptance.
Warren Wiersbe

True faith does not so much attempt to
manipulate God to do our will as it does
to position us to do his will.
Philip Yancey

When things happen which dismay, we ought
to look to God for His meaning and remember
that He is not taken by surprise nor can His
purposes be thwarted in the end.
Elisabeth Elliot

I FIND THAT DOING THE WILL OF GOD LEAVES ME NO TIME FOR DISPUTING HIS PLANS.

George MacDonald

FAITH WILL NOT ALWAYS GET FOR US WHAT WE WANT, BUT IT WILL GET WHAT GOD WANTS US TO HAVE.

Vance Havner

"THE LORD IS MY ROCK, AND MY FORTRESS, AND MY DELIVERER; MY GOD, MY STRENGTH, IN WHOM I WILL TRUST . . . ."

Psalm 18:2 KJV

CHAPTER 3: FAITH THROUGH OBEDIENCE

FAITH

FRIENDS

FAMILY

Now faith is the substance of things hoped for, the evidence of things not seen. Hebrews 11:1 NKJV

FITNESS

FUN

Obedience to God is the hallmark of a well-lived life. But sometimes, obedience to God is difficult indeed. We live in a world that is filled to the brim with distractions and temptations. Our challenge, despite these enticements, is to live according to the principles found in God's Holy Word.

Life is a series of decisions and choices. Each day, we make countless decisions that can bring us closer to God...or not. When we live according to God's Word, we earn for ourselves the abundance and peace He intends for our lives.

Do you seek God's peace and His blessings? Then obey Him. When you're faced with a difficult choice or a powerful temptation, seek God's counsel and trust the counsel He gives. Invite God into your heart and live according to His Word. When you do, you will be blessed today, tomorrow, and forever.

"SHOW ME YOUR FAITH WITHOUT YOUR WORKS, AND I WILL SHOW YOU MY FAITH BY MY WORKS."

James 2:18 NKJV

Obedience is the key of knowledge.
Christina Rossetti

For almighty God willeth that we be perfectly
subject and obedient to him and that
we rise high above our own will and above
our own reason by a great burning love
and a whole desire for him.
Thomas á Kempis

Only he who believes is obedient,
and only he who is obedient believes.
Dietrich Bonhoeffer

Obedience is the outward expression
of your love of God.
Henry Blackaby

Let us remember therefore this lesson: That to
worship our God sincerely we must evermore
begin by hearkening to His voice, and by
giving ear to what He commands us. For if
every man goes after his own way, we shall
wander. We may well run, but we shall
never be a whit nearer to the right way,
but rather farther away from it.
John Calvin

God uses ordinary people who are obedient
to Him to do extraordinary things.
John Maxwell

Make this day a day of obedience,
a day of spiritual joy, and a day of peace.
Make this day's work a little part of
the work of the Kingdom of my Lord Christ.
John Baillie

HAPPINESS IS OBEDIENCE, AND OBEDIENCE IS HAPPINESS.

C. H. Spurgeon

Let your fellowship with the Father
and with the Lord Jesus Christ have as its one
aim and object a life of quiet, determined,
unquestioning obedience.
Andrew Murray

God's love for His children in unconditional,
no strings attached. But, God's blessings on
our lives do come with a condition—
obedience. If we are to receive the fullness of
God's blessings, we must obey Him
and keep His commandments.
Jim Gallery

Rejoicing is a matter of obedience to God—
an obedience that will start you on
the road to peace and contentment.
Kay Arthur

Do something that demonstrates faith,
for faith with no effort is no faith at all.
Max Lucado

When we choose deliberately to obey Him,
then He will tax the remotest star
and the last grain of sand to assist us
with all His almighty power.
Oswald Chambers

I know the power obedience has for making
things easy which seem impossible.
St. Teresa of Avila

The simple fact is that if we sow a lifestyle
that is in direct disobedience to God's reveled
Word, we ultimately reap disaster.
Charles Swindoll

Don't worry about what you do not
understand. Worry about what you do
understand in the Bible but do not live by.
Corrie ten Boom

If we have the true love of God in our hearts,
we will show it in our lives. We will not have
to go up and down the earth proclaiming it.
We will show it in everything we say or do.
D. L. Moody

GOD'S MARK IS ON EVERYTHING THAT OBEYS HIM.

Martin Luther

"THEREFORE WHOEVER HEARS THESE SAYINGS OF MINE, AND DOES THEM, I WILL LIKEN HIM TO A WISE MAN WHO BUILT HIS HOUSE ON THE ROCK: AND THE RAIN DESCENDED, THE FLOODS CAME, AND THE WINDS BLEW AND BEAT ON THAT HOUSE; AND IT DID NOT FALL, FOR IT WAS FOUNDED ON THE ROCK."

Matthew 7:24-25 NKJV

CHAPTER 4: FAITH IN THE FUTURE

FAITH

FRIENDS

FAMILY

For I know the thoughts that I think toward you, says the LORD, thoughts of peace and not of evil, to give you a future and a hope.
Jeremiah 29:11 NKJV

FITNESS

FUN

Ours is an uncertain world. But of this we can be certain: when we place our faith in God and His only begotten Son, our own future is secure.

When we trust God, we must trust Him without reservation. We must steel ourselves against the inevitable disappointments of the day, secure in the knowledge our Heavenly Father has a plan for the future we cannot see.

Can you place your future into the hands of a loving and all-knowing God? Can you live amid the uncertainties of today, knowing God has dominion over all your tomorrows? If you can, you are wise and you are blessed. When you trust God with everything you are and everything you have, He will give you strength and life, not just for today, but for all eternity.

The Lord Himself has laid the foundation of His people's hopes. We must determine if our hopes are built on this foundation.
C. H. Spurgeon

Be kindly affectioned one to another with brotherly love; in honor preferring one another; not slothful in business; fervent in spirit; serving the Lord; rejoicing in hope; patient in tribulation; continuing instant in prayer . . . .
Romans 12:10-12 KJV

Keep your feet on the ground, but let your heart soar as high as it will. Refuse to be average or to surrender to the chill of your spiritual environment.
A. W. Tozer

If our hearts have been attuned to God
through an abiding faith in Christ,
the result will be joyous optimism
and good cheer.
Billy Graham

When you say a situation or a person
is hopeless, you are slamming the door
in the face of God.
Charles Allen

Do not limit the limitless God!
With Him, face the future unafraid
because you are never alone.
Mrs. Charles E. Cowman

**DO NOT BUILD UP
OBSTACLES IN YOUR
IMAGINATION.
DIFFICULTIES MUST BE
STUDIED AND DEALT
WITH, BUT THEY MUST
NOT BE MAGNIFIED
BY FEAR.**

Norman Vincent Peale

Without faith nothing is possible.
With it, nothing is impossible.
Mary McLeod Bethune

Make yourselves nests of pleasant thoughts.
John Ruskin

Reflect upon your blessings, of which
every man has plenty, not on your past
misfortunes, of which all men have some.
Charles Dickens

Take courage. We walk in the wilderness
today and in the Promised Land tomorrow.
D. L. Moody

The essence of optimism is that it takes no
account of the present, but it is a source of
inspiration, of vitality, and of hope.
Where others have resigned, it enables
a man to hold his head high, to claim
the future for himself, and
not abandon it to his enemy.
Dietrich Bonhoeffer

Never be afraid to trust an unknown future
to a known God.
Corrie ten Boom

HOPE MUST BE IN THE FUTURE
TENSE. FAITH, TO BE FAITH,
MUST ALWAYS BE IN
THE PRESENT TENSE.

Catherine Marshall

"NOW FAITH IS
THE SUBSTANCE
OF THINGS HOPED FOR,
THE EVIDENCE OF THINGS
NOT SEEN."

Hebrews 11:1 KJV

F AS IN FAMILY

FAITH

FRIENDS

FAMILY

If we love one another, God abides in us, and His love has been perfected in us.
1 John 4:12 NKJV

FITNESS

FUN

FAMILY

The second factor for successful living is family. Your family is God's gift to you. He expects you to treat His gift with care, dignity, respect, and, above all, love.

My wife and boys are truly blessings. Since the day they were born I have tried to end each day as they go to bed by telling the boys "You are my gift from God." I am not perfect, and have hurt and disappointed them at times. But I strive to be the best husband and dad I can be. I look to the heavenly Father as the perfect example.

Build your lives and families on the rock that cannot be shaken . . . trust in your Creator. When we place God squarely in the center of our families'—when we worship Him, praise Him, trust Him, and love Him—then God will bless us in ways we could have scarcely imagined.

CHAPTER 5: THE GIFT OF LOVE

FAITH

FRIENDS

FAMILY

And now abide faith, hope, love, these three; but the greatest of these is love.
1 Corinthians 13:13 NKJV

FITNESS

FUN

The familiar words of 1st Corinthians 13:13 remind us of the importance of love. Faith is important, of course. So, too, is hope. But, love is more important still.

Love is at the foundation of successful family life. When we express our love genuinely and often—and when we express that love not just with our words but also with our actions—we honor the One who first loved us.

Christ showed His love for us on the cross, and, as Christians, we are called upon to return Christ's love by sharing it. Today, let us share Christ's love to all who need it, starting with that little band of parents, grandparents, kids, and grandkids God has placed under our care.

THE FIRST ESSENTIAL FOR A HAPPY HOME IS LOVE.

Billy Graham

The only true source of meaning in life
is found in love for God and his son
Jesus Christ, and love for mankind,
beginning with our own families.
James Dobson

As the family goes, so goes the nation
and so goes the whole world in which we live.
Pope John Paul II

You always win a better response with love.
Helen Hosier

Let us look upon our children; let us love
them and train them as children of
the covenant and children of the promise.
These are the children of God.
Andrew Murray

Children are not so different from kites.
Children were created to fly. But, they need
wind, the undergirding, and strength
that comes from unconditional love,
encouragement, and prayer.
Gigi Graham Tchividjian

*And this commandment we have from Him:
that he who loves God must love
his brother also.*
1 John 4:21 NKJV

When God measures a man,
He puts the tape around the heart
instead of the head.
Anonymous

Brotherly love is still the distinguishing badge
of every true Christian.
Matthew Henry

Give me such love for God and men
as will blot out all hatred and bitterness.
Dietrich Bonhoeffer

"LET LOVE BE WITHOUT
HYPOCRISY.
ABHOR WHAT IS EVIL.
CLING TO WHAT IS
GOOD. BE KINDLY
AFFECTIONATE TO
ONE ANOTHER WITH
BROTHERLY LOVE,
IN HONOR GIVING
PREFERENCE TO
ONE ANOTHER."

Romans 12:9-10 NKJV

HOMES THAT ARE BUILT ON ANYTHING OTHER THAN LOVE ARE BOUND TO CRUMBLE.
Billy Graham

"BELOVED, IF GOD SO LOVED US, WE ALSO OUGHT TO LOVE ONE ANOTHER."
1 John 4:11 NKJV

CHAPTER 6: THE GIFT OF TIME

FAITH

FRIENDS

To everything there is a season, and a time to every purpose under heaven.
Ecclesiastes 3:1 KJV

FITNESS

FUN

In this fast-paced world, distractions can be numerous and obligations can be unrelenting. If you're like many of us, your schedule is filled with things to do and places to be. Despite these demands, you *can* and *should* invest much of your day in the "care and feeding" of your family. To do otherwise is to forfeit one of life's greatest joys.

Your family deserves substantial blocks of uninterrupted time *with you*. *You* deserve the rewards which come from those special, unexpected moments that happen *only* when you and your loved ones share time together.

God intends you invest your time and energy in the care and nurturing of your clan. When you do, He will bless you and your family in ways beyond your wildest imagination.

Children just don't fit into a "to do" list very
well. It takes time to be an effective parent
when children are small. It takes time to
introduce them to good books—it takes time
to fly kites and play punch ball and put
together jigsaw puzzles. It takes time to listen.
James Dobson

Happy is the child who happens in upon
his parent from time to time to see him on
his knees, or going aside regularly,
to keep times with the Lord.
Larry Christenson

I have decided not to let my time be used up
by people to whom I make no difference
while I neglect those for whom
I am irreplaceable.
Tony Campolo

NEVER GIVE YOUR FAMILY THE LEFTOVERS AND CRUMBS OF YOUR TIME.

Charles Swindoll

You have heard about "quality time" and
"quantity time." Your family needs both.
Jim Gallery

Lost time is never found again.
Ben Franklin

What we love to do we find time to do.
John L. Spalding

BALANCE WISELY YOUR PROFESSIONAL LIFE AND YOUR FAMILY LIFE. GOD ONLY ALLOWS US SO MANY OPPORTUNITIES WITH OUR CHILDREN TO READ A STORY, TO GO FISHING, TO PLAY CATCH, AND TO SAY OUR PRAYERS TOGETHER. TRY NOT TO MISS A SINGLE ONE OF THEM.

James Dobson

"I TRUST IN YOU, O LORD; I SAY, 'YOU ARE MY GOD.' MY TIMES ARE IN YOUR HAND."

Psalm 31:14-15 NKJV

CHAPTER 7: COURTESY, CONSIDERATION, & CARING

FAITH

FRIENDS

FAMILY

And be kind to one another, tenderhearted, forgiving one another, even as God in Christ forgave you.
Ephesians 4:32 NKJV

FITNESS

FUN

Did Christ instruct us in matters of etiquette and courtesy? Of course He did. Christ's instructions are clear: " Therefore, whatever you want men to do to you, do also to them, for this is the Law and the Prophets." (Matthew 7:12 NKJV). Jesus did not say, "In some things, treat people as you wish to be treated." And He did not say, "From time to time, treat others with kindness." Christ said we should treat others as we wish to be treated in every aspect of our daily lives.

Common courtesy should begin at home. So today, be a little kinder than necessary to everyone you meet, starting with your family. As you consider all the things Christ has done in your life, honor Him with your words and deeds. He expects no less. He deserves no less.

YOU WILL ACCOMPLISH MORE BY KIND WORDS AND A COURTEOUS MANNER THAN BY ANGER AND SHARP REBUKE, WHICH SHOULD NEVER BE USED, EXCEPT IN NECESSITY.

St. Angela Merici

The Golden Rule begins at home.
Marie T. Freeman

There is nothing that rejuvenates
the parched, delicate spirits of children faster
than when a lighthearted spirit pervades
the home and laughter fills its halls.
James Dobson

Anything done for another is done for oneself.
Pope John Paul II

When you extend hospitality to others,
you're not trying to impress people;
you're trying to reflect God to them.
Max Lucado

People don't care how much you know
until they know how much you care.
John Maxwell

"PLEASANT WORDS ARE LIKE A HONEYCOMB. SWEETNESS TO THE SOUL AND HEALTH TO THE BONES."

Proverbs 16:24 NKJV

THE NICEST THING WE CAN DO FOR OUR HEAVENLY FATHER IS TO BE KIND TO ONE OF HIS CHILDREN.

St. Teresa of Avila

**TOO OFTEN WE
UNDERESTIMATE THE POWER
OF A TOUCH, A SMILE, A KIND
WORD, A LISTENING EAR,
AN HONEST COMPLIMENT, OR
THE SMALLEST ACT OF CARING,
ALL OF WHICH HAVE
THE POTENTIAL TO
TURN A LIFE AROUND.**

Leo Buscaglia

**"DO NOT FORGET TO
ENTERTAIN STRANGERS, FOR
BY SO DOING SOME PEOPLE
HAVE ENTERTAINED ANGELS
WITHOUT KNOWING IT."**

Hebrews 13:2 NIV

F AS IN FITNESS

FRIENDS

FAITH

FAMILY

Do you not know that you are the temple of God and that the Spirit of God dwells in you?
1 Corinthians 3:16 NKJV

FITNESS

FUN

FITNESS

The third "F" is for fitness. God has given each of us a single body that is ours to use during this lifetime; He has instructed us to use that body with care. Yet in today's world, we may be sorely tempted to do otherwise.

Ours is a world in which food is plentiful and work is often sedentary. When calories are cheap and exercise is optional, too many of us neglect to care for our bodies. In failing to do so, we pay a terrible high price.

This is an area I struggle with. I have suffered the consequences of not taking care of myself. Thankfully I have had the chance to "regroup" and get in better shape, but it is still a battle. I am comforted by the thought that healthy living is a journey, not a destination. As long as you are moving towards better health, the occasional misstep can be overcome. If you're willing to make the step-by-step journey toward improved health, rest assured God is taking careful note of your progress . . . and He's quietly urging you to take the next step.

CHAPTER 8:
COMMON SENSE, UNCOMMON HEALTH

FAITH

FRIENDS

FAMILY

But those who wait on the Lord Shall renew their strength; They shall mount up with wings like eagles, They shall run and not be weary, They shall walk and not faint. Isaiah 40:31 NKJV

FITNESS

FUN

Health is a gift from God. What we do with that gift is determined, to a surprising extent, by the person we see every time we gaze into the mirror. If we squander our health—or if we take it for granted—we do a profound disservice to ourselves and our loved ones. But God has other plans. He commands us to treat our bodies, our minds, and our souls with the utmost care. And that's exactly what we should do.

Do you sincerely seek to care for the body God has given you? If so, a good place to start is with the application of good old-fashioned common sense. For starters: eat sensibly, exercise regularly, and see your doctor once a year, even if you're not sick. And one more thing: laugh often!

LAUGHTER IS, BY DEFINITION, HEALTHY.

Doris Lessing

The three great essentials to achieve anything
worthwhile are: first, hard work; second,
stick-to-itiveness; third, common sense.
Thomas Edison

Look to your health; and if you have it,
praise God and value it next to conscience;
for health is the second blessing
that we mortals are capable of,
a blessing money can't buy.
Izaak Walton

Our body is like armor, our soul like
the warrior. Take care of both, and
you will be ready for what comes.
Amma St. Syncletica

"BELOVED, I PRAY THAT YOU MAY PROSPER IN ALL THINGS AND BE IN HEALTH, JUST AS YOUR SOUL PROSPERS."

3 John 1:2 NKJV

THE FIRST WEALTH
IS HEALTH.

Ralph Waldo Emerson

The best doctors in the world are
Doctor Diet, Doctor Quiet,
and Dr. Merryman.
Jonathan Swift

Liberty is to the collective body,
what health is to every individual body.
Without health no pleasure can be tasted
by man; without liberty, no happiness
can be enjoyed by society.
Henry IV

Birds which are too heavy cannot fly
very high. The same is true of those
who mistreat their bodies.
St. John Climacus

People who cannot find time
for recreation are obliged sooner
or later to find time for illness.
John Wanamaker

Sleep is the golden chain that ties
health and our bodies together.
Thomas Dekker

Taking care of yourself physically really helps
emotionally. People who get a lot of sleep,
who do the things that relieve stress,
can withstand a lot of stress.
Laura Bush

EARLY TO BED AND EARLY TO RISE, MAKES A MAN HEALTHY, WEALTHY, AND WISE.

Ben Franklin

ABSTINENCE IS THE MOTHER OF HEALTH. A FEW OUNCES OF GOING WITHOUT IS AN EXCELLENT RECIPE FOR EVERY AILMENT.

Anthony Grassi

"I SHALL YET PRAISE HIM, WHO IS THE HEALTH OF MY COUNTENANCE, AND MY GOD."

Psalm 42:11 KJV

I HAVE MADE A CONTRACT WITH
MY BODY: IT HAS PROMISED
TO ACCEPT HARSH TREATMENT
FROM ME ON EARTH, AND
I HAVE PROMISED THAT IT
SHALL RECEIVE ETERNAL
REST IN HEAVEN.

St. Peter of Alcantara

"WHATSOEVER THY HAND
FINDETH TO DO,
DO IT WITH THY MIGHT."

Ecclesiastes 9:10 KJV

CHAPTER 9: REST & RENEWAL

FAITH

FRIENDS

FAMILY

Come unto me, all ye that labor and are heavy laden, and I will give you rest.
Matthew 11:28 KJV

FITNESS

FUN

Are you burning your candle at both ends? If so, welcome to the club: ours is a very busy world filled with very weary people. But if you think God *intends* for you to rush through life with your spiritual batteries drained, you're wrong. God promises rest, renewal, and abundance to those who genuinely seek His presence. Your task, of course, is to slow down long enough to accept God's gifts.

If the demands of daily life are robbing you of the joy that is rightfully yours in Christ, it's high time to pause and have a private talk with your Heavenly Father. When you do, you'll discover the truth of Isaiah 40:31: "But those who wait on the Lord Shall renew their strength; They shall mount up with wings like eagles; They shall run and not be weary; They shall walk and not faint" (NKJV).

In other words, the Creator of the universe stands always ready and always able to create a new sense of wonderment and joy in you *if* you let Him. So why not let Him today?

LIFE IS STRENUOUS.
SEE THAT YOUR CLOCK
DOES NOT RUN DOWN.

Mrs. Charles E. Cowman

Jesus gives us the ultimate rest,
the confidence we need, to escape
the frustration and chaos of
the world around us.
Billy Graham

Father, for this day, renew within me
the gift of the Holy Spirit.
Andrew Murray

He is the God of wholeness and restoration.
Stormie Omartian

**JESUS IS CALLING
THE WEARY TO REST,
CALLING TODAY,
CALLING TODAY,
BRING HIM YOUR
BURDEN AND YOU
SHALL BE BLEST;
HE WILL NOT TURN
YOU AWAY.**

Fanny Crosby

God is not running an antique shop!
He is making all things new!
Vance Havner

With God, it's never "Plan B" or
"second best." It's always "Plan A."
And, if we let Him, He'll make
something beautiful of our lives.
Gloria Gaither

I wish I could make it all new again; I can't.
But God can. "He restores my soul,"
wrote the shepherd. God doesn't reform;
he restores. He doesn't camouflage the old;
he restores the new. The Master Builder will
pull out the original plan and restore it.
He will restore the vigor, he will restore
the energy. He will restore the hope.
He will restore the soul.
Max Lucado

MOST OF MAN'S TROUBLE COMES FROM HIS INABILITY TO BE STILL.

Blaise Pascal

JESUS, MY SAVIOR, LOOK ON ME, FOR I AM WEARY AND OPPRESSED; I COME TO CAST MYSELF ON THEE: THOU ART MY REST.

Charlotte Elliott

With every rising of the sun,
think of your life as just begun.
Anonymous

Although no one can go back and
make a brand new start, anyone can start
from now and make a brand new end.
Harvey Mackay

Resolutely slam and lock the door on
past sin and failure, and throw away the key.
Oswald Chambers

**PRESCRIPTION FOR
A HAPPIER AND
HEALTHIER LIFE:
RESOLVE TO SLOW
DOWN YOUR PACE;
LEARN TO SAY "NO"
GRACEFULLY; RESIST
THE TEMPTATION
TO CHASE AFTER
MORE PLEASURE,
MORE HOBBIES,
AND MORE SOCIAL
ENTANGLEMENTS.**

James Dobson

BIRDS SING AFTER THE STORM. WHY SHOULDN'T WE?

Rose Kennedy

**WORK IS NOT ALWAYS
REQUIRED OF A MAN.
THERE IS SUCH A THING
AS SACRED IDLENESS,
THE CULTIVATION OF WHICH
IS NOW FEARFULLY
NEGLECTED.**

George MacDonald

**"CREATE IN ME
A CLEAN HEART,
O GOD, AND RENEW
A STEADFAST SPIRIT
WITHIN ME."**

Psalm 51:10 NKJV

F AS IN FRIENDS

FAITH

FRIENDS

FAMILY

Iron sharpeneth iron; so a man sharpeneth the countenance of his friend.
Proverbs 27:17 KJV

FITNESS

FUN

FRIENDS

The fourth "F" is for friendship. Loyal Christian friendship is ordained by God. Throughout the Bible, we are reminded to love one another, to care for one another, and to treat one another as we wish to be treated. As you journey through the day ahead, remember the important role Christian friendship plays in God's plans for His kingdom *and* for your life.

I have been blessed with incredible friends—Christian brothers. Some I see regularly, some have been distanced by time. But that distance closes with light-speed when we get reconnected or a need arises in the other's life. Mike, Dave, Cliff, Kerry, Bill, Tim, Scott, Ron, and many others, are true blessings from God to me.

Christ promises His followers that through Him they may experience abundance (John 10:10). May your friends bless you abundantly, and may you do the same for them. Take time to connect with old friends, or make new ones.

CHAPTER 10: THE GIFT OF FRIENDSHIP

FAITH

FRIENDS

FAMILY

How good and pleasant it is when brothers live together in unity!
Psalm 133:1 NIV

FITNESS

FUN

Jesus is the sovereign friend and ultimate Savior of mankind. Christ showed His love for believers by willingly sacrificing His own life, that we might have eternal life. We, as Christ's followers, are challenged to share His love.

When we accept Christ as our Savior, we become ambassadors for Him (2 Corinthians 5:20). When we walk each day with Jesus—and obey the commandments found in God's Holy Word—we are not only worthy ambass-adors, we are also trustworthy friends.

The words of John 15:13 remind us that, "Greater love hath no man than this, that a man lay down his life for his friends" (KJV). Such is Christ's love for us. When we share that love, we share a priceless gift. As loyal friends, we must do no less.

The best times in life are made
a thousand times better when shared
with a dear friend.
Luci Swindoll

A true friend is the gift of God,
and only He who made hearts
can unite them.
Robert South

Friendship is the source of
the greatest pleasures, and without friends
even the most agreeable pursuits
become tedious.
St. Thomas Aquinas

IN FRIENDSHIP, GOD OPENS YOUR EYES TO THE GLORIES OF HIMSELF.

Joni Eareckson Tada

A friend is the hope of the heart.
Ralph Waldo Emerson

Few sounds on earth can compare with
the reverberations of friends
laughing together.
Criswell Freeman

I have found that the closer I am to
the godly people around me, the easier it is
for me to live a righteous life because
they hold me accountable.
John MacArthur

Few delights can equal the mere presence
of one whom we trust utterly.
George MacDonald

My friends have made the story of my life.
In a thousand ways they have turned
my limitations into beautiful privileges
and enabled me to walk serene and happy in
the shadow cast by my deprivation.
Helen Keller

A friend is one who makes me do my best.
Oswald Chambers

Whenever we develop significant friendships
with those who are not like us culturally,
we become broader, wiser persons.
Richard Foster

Don't bypass the potential for meaningful
friendships just because of differences.
Explore them. Embrace them. Love them.
Luci Swindoll

Friends are angels who lift our feet
when our own wings have trouble
remembering how to fly.
Anonymous

"STAY"
IS A CHARMING WORD
IN A FRIEND'S
VOCABULARY.

Louisa May Alcott

We long to find someone who has been
where we've been, who shares our fragile
skies, who sees our sunsets
with the same shades of blue.
Beth Moore

Friendship is one of the sweetest joys of life.
Many might have failed beneath
the bitterness of their trial had they
not found a friend.
C. H. Spurgeon

God has not called us to see through
each other, but to see each other through.
Jess Moody

**FRIENDSHIP IS UNNECESSARY,
LIKE PHILOSOPHY, LIKE ART.
IT HAS NO SURVIVAL VALUE;
RATHER IT IS ONE OF THOSE
THINGS THAT GIVE VALUE
TO SURVIVAL.**

C. S. Lewis

**"I THANK MY GOD EVERY TIME
I REMEMBER YOU."**

Philippians 1:3 NIV

CHAPTER 11: THE ART OF FRIENDSHIP

FAITH

FRIENDS

FAMILY

And let us not be weary in well doing: for in due season we shall reap, if we faint not.
Galatians 6:9 KJV

FITNESS

FUN

In *The Message*, Eugene Peterson retells the Golden Rule as follows: "Here is a simple, rule-of-thumb for behavior: Ask yourself what you want people to do for you, then grab the initiative and do it for them. Add up God's Law and Prophets and this is what you get" (Matthew 7:12 MSG). Not surprisingly, the Golden Rule for life is also the Golden Rule for friendship. We must do unto others as we would have them do unto us. Period.

Because we are imperfect human beings, we are, on occasion, selfish, thoughtless, or even cruel. But God commands us to behave otherwise. He teaches us to rise above our own imperfections and to treat others with unselfishness and love. When we observe God's Golden Rule, we help build His kingdom here on earth. When we share the love of Christ, we share a priceless gift. May we share it today, and every day we live.

A FRIEND IS ONE WHO MAKES ME DO MY BEST.

Oswald Chambers

A friend may well be reckoned
a masterpiece of nature.
Ralph Waldo Emerson

Love one another fervently with a pure heart.
1 Peter 1:22 NKJV

The single most important element in
any human relationship is honesty—
with oneself, with God, and with others.
Catherine Marshall

When we honestly ask ourselves which person in our lives means the most to us, we often find that it is he who, instead of giving much advice, solutions, and cures, has chosen rather to share our pain and touch our wounds with a gentle and tender hand. The friend who can be silent with us in a moment of despair or confusion, who can stay with us in an hour of grief and bereavement, who can tolerate not knowing, not curing, not healing, and face us with the reality of our powerlessness, that is a friend who cares.
Henri Nouwen

True friends don't spend time gazing into each other's eyes. They show great tenderness toward each other, but they face in the same direction, toward common projects, interest, goals, and above all, toward a common Lord.
C. S. Lewis

FRIENDSHIP IS A SINGLE SOUL DWELLING IN TWO BODIES.

Aristotle

"A NEW COMMAND I GIVE YOU: LOVE ONE ANOTHER. AS I HAVE LOVED YOU, SO YOU MUST LOVE ONE ANOTHER. BY THIS ALL MEN WILL KNOW YOU ARE MY DISCIPLES, IF YOU LOVE ONE ANOTHER."

John 13:34-35 NIV

Do not protect yourself by a fence,
but rather by your friends.
Czech Proverb

The essence of true friendship is to make
allowance for another's little lapses.
David Storey

When a friend is in trouble, don't annoy him
by asking if there is anything you can do.
Think up something appropriate and do it.
Edgar Watson Howe

Be slow in choosing a friend,
slower in changing.
Ben Franklin

Without loyalty, true friendship is impossible.
But with loyalty, true friendship is inevitable.
Criswell Freeman

Do you want to be wise?
Choose wise friends.
Charles Swindoll

**WE SHOULD BEHAVE TO
OUR FRIENDS AS WE WOULD
WISH OUR FRIENDS
TO BEHAVE TO US.**
Aristotle

**"A FRIEND LOVETH
AT ALL TIMES."**
Proverbs 17:17 KJV

F AS IN FUN

FAITH

FRIENDS

FAMILY

Rejoice in the Lord always. Again I will say, rejoice!
Philippians 4:4 KJV

FITNESS

FUN

FUN

The final "F" stands for fun. As a Christian, you have every reason to celebrate. But God won't force His joys upon you; you must claim them for yourself.

Two thoughts have really struck me lately. First, fun starts by reminding yourself to be a joy-filled Christian! I was reminded of this recently by overhearing a gentleman pray. He and I were both at an airport at an unreasonably early hour. I was moaning about the time, and yet when he prayed it reminded me that fun starts with being Spirit-filled. Are you a living, breathing example of the spiritual abundance Christ offers His believers? Hopefully, you are. Your family and friends need positive role models who clearly demonstrate the trans-forming power of Christ's love. *You* need the experience of rejoicing in the glorious life God has given you.

Second, fun does not just happen to come your way. You have to make it happen. Taking five minutes to wrestle with my youngest boy, ignoring his homework and my work for just a little while, was more fun than I could have imagined.

CHAPTER 12: THIS IS THE DAY

FRIENDS

FAITH

FAMILY

This is the day which the LORD hath made; we will rejoice and be glad in it.
Psalm 118:24 KJV

FUN

FITNESS

The Christian faith should be cause for celebration! God is in His heaven, Christ has risen, and we are the sheep of His flock.

The familiar words of Psalm 118:24 remind us that every day is a gift from God. Yet on some days, we don't feel much like celebrating. When the obligations of everyday living seem to overwhelm us, we may find ourselves frustrated by the demands of the present, and worried by the uncertainty of the future.

Each day is a special treasure to be savored and enjoyed. May we—as believers who have so much to celebrate—never fail to praise our Creator by rejoicing in His glorious creation.

I delight greatly in the LORD;
my soul rejoices in my God.
Isaiah 61:10 NIV

Therefore do not worry about tomorrow,
for tomorrow will worry about its own things.
Sufficient for the day is its own trouble.
Matthew 6:34 NKJV

The one word in the spiritual vocabulary
is now.
Oswald Chambers

Rejoice and be exceedingly glad,
for great is your reward in heaven.
Matthew 5:12 NKJV

He that fears not the future
may enjoy the present.
Thomas Fuller

Do not so contemplate eternity
that you waste today.
Vance Havner

THE FUTURE STARTS TODAY, NOT TOMORROW.

Pope John Paul II

Now is the only time worth having because,
indeed, it is the only time we have.
C. H. Spurgeon

A glimpse of the next three feet of road
is more important and useful
than a view of the horizon.
C. S. Lewis

Love, joy, peace, patience, kindness, goodness,
faithfulness, gentleness, and self-control.
To these I commit my day. If I succeed,
I will give thanks. If I fail, I will seek his
grace. And then, when this day is done,
I will place my head on my pillow and rest.
Max Lucado

EACH DAY, LOOK FOR A KERNEL OF EXCITEMENT.

Barbara Jordan

**WHEREVER YOU ARE,
BE ALL THERE.
LIVE TO THE HILT EVERY
SITUATION YOU BELIEVE
TO BE THE WILL OF GOD.**

Jim Elliot

**"ENCOURAGE ONE ANOTHER
DAILY, AS LONG AS
IT IS CALLED TODAY . . . ."**

Hebrews 3:13 NIV

CHAPTER 13:
CELEBRATING GOD'S CREATION

FAITH

FRIENDS

FAMILY

Then God saw everything that He had made, and indeed it was very good.
Genesis 1:31 NKJV

FITNESS

FUN

Morning by morning, the sun rises upon a breathtaking world filled with God's presence and His love. God's handiwork is indeed glorious to behold. It is our responsibility, as grateful recipients of God's gifts, to appreciate them.

Have you paused today to give thanks for God's wonderful world? If not, it's time to close this book and offer up a prayer of thanksgiving and praise. God made the tiniest grain of sand *and* the most distant star in our universe. His creation is as miraculous as it is beautiful. So pause, look, marvel, and give thanks . . . now and forever, amen!

THE ORDERLY ARRANGEMENT OF THE WHOLE UNIVERSE IS A KIND OF MUSICAL HARMONY WHOSE MAKER AND ARTIST IS GOD.

St. John of Damascus

When we look at the order of creation,
we form in our own minds an image,
not of the essence, but of the wisdom of
Him who has made all things wisely.
St. Gregory of Nyssa

It is great—and there is no other greatness—
to make one nook of
God's creation more fruitful.
Thomas Carlyle

The LORD is gracious and full of compassion,
Slow to anger and great in mercy.
The LORD is good to all,
And His tender mercies are
over all His works.
Psalm 145:8-9 NKJV

O God, Thou hast made us for Thyself,
and our hearts are restless
until they find their rest in Thee.
St. Augustine

Jesus Christ is the first and last, author and
finisher, beginning and end, alpha and omega,
and by Him all other things hold together.
He must be first or nothing.
God never comes next!
Vance Havner

I love to think of nature as an unlimited
broadcasting station through which
God speaks to us every hour—if we will
only tune in.
George Washington Carver

Heaven and earth and all that is in
the universe cry out to me from all directions
that I, O God, must love You.
St. Augustine

God is the silent partner
in all great enterprises.
Abraham Lincoln

*He is the image of the invisible God,
the firstborn over all creation. For by Him
all things were created that are in heaven
and that are on earth, visible and invisible,
whether thrones or dominions
or principalities or powers. All things
were created through Him and for Him.*
Colossians 1:15-16 NKJV

GOD DID NOT SPRING FORTH FROM ETERNITY; HE BROUGHT FORTH ETERNITY.

C. H. Spurgeon

NO PHILOSOPHICAL THEORY
WHICH I HAVE YET COME
ACROSS IS A RADICAL
IMPROVEMENT ON THE WORDS
OF GENESIS, THAT "IN THE
BEGINNING GOD MADE
HEAVEN AND EARTH."

C. S. Lewis

"FOR HE CHOSE US IN HIM
BEFORE THE CREATION OF
THE WORLD TO BE HOLY AND
BLAMELESS IN HIS SIGHT.
IN LOVE HE PREDESTINED US
TO BE ADOPTED AS HIS SONS
THROUGH JESUS CHRIST,
IN ACCORDANCE WITH HIS
PLEASURE AND WILL . . . ."

Ephesians 1:4-5 NIV

CHAPTER 14: THE JOYFUL CHRISTIAN

FAITH

FRIENDS

FAMILY

Rejoice evermore. Pray without ceasing. In every thing give thanks: for this is the will of God in Christ Jesus concerning you.
1 Thessalonians 5:16-18 KJV

FITNESS

FUN

Is your faith a cause for celebration? It should be. Christ made it clear to His followers: He intended His joy would become their joy. It still holds true today: Christ intends His believers share His love with joy in their hearts. Yet sometimes, amid the inevitable hustle and bustle of life-here-on-earth, we can forfeit—albeit tempor-arily—the joy of Christ, as we wrestle with the challenges of daily living.

C. H. Spurgeon, the renowned 19th century English clergymen, advised, "The Lord is glad to open the gate to every knocking soul. It opens very freely; its hinges are not rusted; no bolts secure it. Have faith and enter at this moment through holy courage. If you knock with a heavy heart, you shall yet sing with joy of spirit. Never be discouraged!"

If, today, your heart is heavy, open the door of your soul to Christ. He will give you peace and joy. If you already have the joy of Christ in your heart, share it freely, as Christ freely shared His joy with you.

God has charged Himself with full
responsibility for our eternal happiness
and stands ready to take over
the management of our lives
the moment we turn in faith to Him.
A. W. Tozer

Make God's will the focus of your life
day by day. If you seek to please Him
and Him alone, you'll find yourself
satisfied with life.
Kay Arthur

Spiritual joy and happiness are the surest sign
of divine grace in the soul.
St. Bonaventure

True contentment comes from godliness in
the heart, not from wealth in the hand.
Warren Wiersbe

A cheerful heart is good medicine . . . .
Proverbs 17:22 NIV

Unparalleled joy and victory come
from allowing Christ to do
"the hard thing" with us.
Beth Moore

Holy activity is the mother of holy joy.
C. H. Spurgeon

Joy is the serious business of heaven.
C. S. Lewis

**TODAY, YOU WILL
ENCOUNTER GOD'S
CREATION. WHEN YOU
SEE THE BEAUTY
AROUND YOU, LET EACH
DETAIL REMIND YOU
TO LIFT YOUR HEAD
IN PRAISE.**

Max Lucado

THE TRUE JOY OF A MAN'S LIFE IS IN HIS RELATIONSHIP TO GOD.

Oswald Chambers

I choose joy. I will refuse the temptation to be
cynical; cynicism is the tool of a lazy thinker.
I will refuse to see people as anything less
than human beings, created by God.
I will refuse to see any problem as anything
less than an opportunity to see God.
Max Lucado

Joy is the characteristic by which God uses
us to re-make the distressing into the desired,
the discarded into the creative.
Joy is prayer—joy is strength—
joy is love—joy is a net of love by
which you can catch souls.
Mother Teresa

THE SUREST MARK OF A CHRISTIAN IS NOT FAITH, OR EVEN LOVE, BUT JOY.

Samuel M. Shoemaker

Christ is not only a remedy for your
weariness and trouble, but he will give you
an abundance of the contrary: joy and delight.
They who come to Christ do not only come
to a resting-place after they have been
wandering in a wilderness, but they come to
a banqueting-house where they may rest,
and where they may feast. They may cease
from their former troubles and toils,
and they may enter upon a course of
delights and spiritual joys.
Jonathan Edwards

*Make a joyful noise unto the LORD,
all ye lands. Serve the LORD with gladness:
come before his presence with singing.*
Psalm 100:1-2 KJV

"DELIGHT THYSELF ALSO IN THE LORD; AND HE SHALL GIVE THEE THE DESIRES OF THINE HEART."

Psalm 37:4 KJV

ABANDON YOURSELF UTTERLY
FOR THE LOVE OF GOD,
AND IN THIS WAY YOU WILL
BECOME TRULY HAPPY.

St. Henry Suso

"HAPPY IS HE . . .
WHOSE HOPE IS IN
THE LORD HIS GOD."

Psalm 146:5 KJV

AND IN CONCLUSION:
THE BALANCED CHRISTIAN LIFE

FAITH

FRIENDS

FAMILY

To everything there is a season, A time for every purpose under heaven. . . .
Ecclesiastes 3:1 NKJV

FITNESS

FUN

The words of James 3:17 remind us "The wisdom that is from above is first pure, then peaceable, gentle, willing to yield, full of mercy and good fruits, without partiality and without hypocrisy" (NKJV). Hopefully, these pages have encouraged you to incorporate God's wisdom, that timeless wisdom that comes from above, into *every* aspect of your life.

If yours is to be a balanced Christian life, you'll make time for the 5 F's: faith, family fitness, friends, and fun. By focusing on these five areas, you will help bring God's abundance to your own life *and* to the lives of your loved ones.

May you welcome God into your heart. May you share His blessings with the world. May you honor Him by making straight F's in the classroom called life.

The Christian is not one who has gone all
the way with Christ. None of us has.
The Christian is one who has found
the right road.
Charles Allen

Have your heart right with Christ,
and he will visit you often, and so turn
weekdays into Sundays, meals into
sacraments, homes into temples,
and earth into heaven.
C. H. Spurgeon

Trusting God is the bottom line
of Christian righteousness.
R. C. Sproul

THE HEART IS RICH WHEN IT IS CONTENT, AND IT IS ALWAYS CONTENT WHEN ITS DESIRES ARE SET UPON GOD.

St. Miguel of Ecuador

The most powerful life is the most simple life.
The most powerful life is the life that knows
where it's going, that knows where the source
of strength is; it is the life that stays free of
clutter and happenstance and hurriedness.
Max Lucado

The life of strain is difficult. The life of
inner peace—a life that comes from
a positive attitude—is the easiest
type of existence.
Norman Vincent Peale

True contentment comes from godliness
in the heart, not from wealth in the hand.
Warren Wiersbe

OUR SENSE OF JOY, SATISFACTION, AND FULFILLMENT IN LIFE INCREASES, NO MATTER WHAT THE CIRCUMSTANCES, IF WE ARE IN THE CENTER OF GOD'S WILL.

Billy Graham

"BECAUSE OF THE LORD'S GREAT LOVE WE ARE NOT CONSUMED, FOR HIS COMPASSIONS NEVER FAIL. THEY ARE NEW EVERY MORNING; GREAT IS YOUR FAITHFULNESS."

Lamentations 3:22-23 NIV

DAVID M. BROWNE

Mr. Browne has recently come out of retirement and accepted the position of President/CEO of Family Christian Stores, the nation's largest retailer of Christian products with over 300 stores nationwide. Prior to this, he spent 2 ½ years actively involved in ministry work, particularly with Athletes in Action (Campus Crusade for Christ's sports ministry), where he serves as Chairman of the Board of Trustees. Previously, he served as CEO of LensCrafters from 1990 through 1999, when he retired.

During his tenure, he helped LensCrafters grow nearly tenfold into the world's largest optical company while building a unique service culture that was recognized by *Fortune* magazine as one of the Top 100 companies to work for, and by the White House for its Gift of Sight philanthropy work.

Dave and his wife, Debbie, are blessed with two children.

Portions of Dave's profits from the proceeds of this book will go to help build the James Fund. The James Fund is a Family Christian Stores' charitable program that assists orphans and widows in the communities where there are Family Christian Stores locations.